This Moment

MIGRATION EDITIONS

Photography by

Lisa Kristine

Published by Migration Editions
4316 Redwood Hwy, Suite 100
San Rafael, California 94903
Edited by Andrea Hamilton, Alameda, California
Designed by 2M Creative, San Francisco, California

Library of Congress Cataloging in Publication Data

Lisa Kristine, 1965 –
This Moment / Lisa Kristine; editor, Andrea Hamilton

ISBN 13: 978-0-9794159-0-6
ISBN 10: 0-9794159-0-X

Printed in People's Republic of China

THIS MOMENT

DEDICATED TO MY MOTHER & FAMILY

ARTIST STATEMENT

In December of 2005, while in North Africa, I was traveling with a caravan of nomadic Tuareg, deep in the dunes of the Great Sahara. This was my third opportunity to spend time and work with these fine people.

The days were meditatively long as we walked across the desert expanse. One late afternoon, the heavy sun was exquisite as it began to sink toward the horizon. The particles of sand transformed from a stunning yellow into a glowing amber hue. We'd been walking for hours, and the winter temperature began to drop quickly—it was time for me to separate from the caravan and begin again to work.

Concerned about losing the luminous light, I traversed the dunes with my equipment, moving as fast as possible against the strong desert wind until I finally arrived at the vantage point I wanted. Standing in this ocean of sand, I felt dwarfed by the dunes reaching as high as one thousand feet. I spread out a large cloth on the sand and began to assemble my view camera. I made a light reading and wrapped my focusing cloth around myself and the camera, studying the scene and holding tightly to the cloth and tripod to keep them from blowing over. Then I waited.

In the distance I could see the caravan of indigo-swathed nomads and their camels climbing the great dunes. As they emerged from behind a wall of sand, I made the first exposure. Then I gathered my equipment and started running to the next location, where I set up again, composed the scene, focused, metered the light, loaded the film, and made another exposure. Within twenty minutes I repeated this process five times and exposed a total of five sheets of film—then the light was gone.

Our world is constantly changing, and I am drawn to cultures vulnerable to this. Modernity is spreading like wild fire, diluting old customs. Before they vanish I want to document them. In 2007 I was in China, working with one of the last remaining women with bound feet—an ancient practice outlawed in 1911. As I said goodbye to Li, a 93-year-old woman whom I had just photographed, she said, "When you come back to China, I probably won't be here." Like her, the rest of the old women with bound feet will be gone soon. In Africa, some hunters and gatherers wear T-shirts instead of goat-skins; in Tibet, Gortex jackets are fast replacing sheep-skin coats; neon storefronts displace ancient brick architecture in Kathmandu. Globalization is here.

My photography is more than work, more than an artistic process. It is all–encompassing; it shapes my soul. It has taught me greater tolerance and respect, and prompted me to reach out my hand to others. When I document and spend time with these individuals, I experience admiration, awe, and amazement. I only hope my work reflects the integrity of these people and all that they have given me.

Having traveled to some 60 countries, I observe that differences—ethnicity, race, religion, culture—tend to foster apprehension, if not hostility, between nations and peoples. I can't help but wonder how different the world could be if distrust were replaced by curiosity, if instead of fear we felt a sense of wonder about others and their differences.

Imagery is a vehicle to transform the boundaries of the mind and be transported immediately into a mood, state or feeling; I hope those who view my work are touched in this way. I hope they are moved by the people gazing back at them and, in that moment, they experience something vital: a simple human connection.

– LISA KRISTINE

Plate 1

HIGH PLATEAU

Tibet

Plate 2 »

DUNES

Morocco

Plate 3

STRIPES

Rif Mountains, Morocco

Plate 4

ARCHES

Meknes, Morocco

Plate 5
SILVER
Northern Thailand

Plate 6

LEANING POTS

India

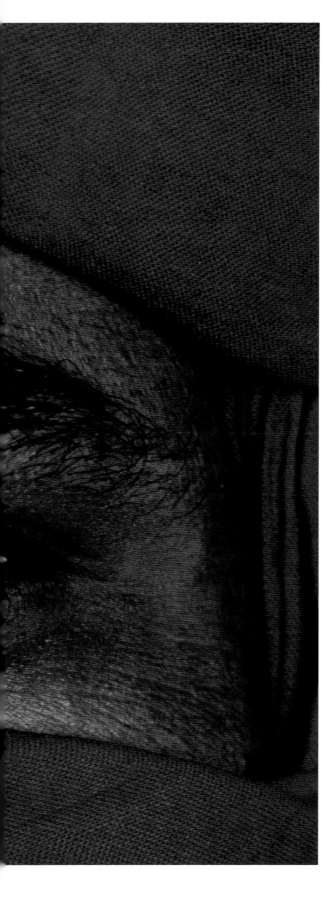

Plate 7

BLUE MAN
Sahara

Plate 8

HOLY BATHER

India

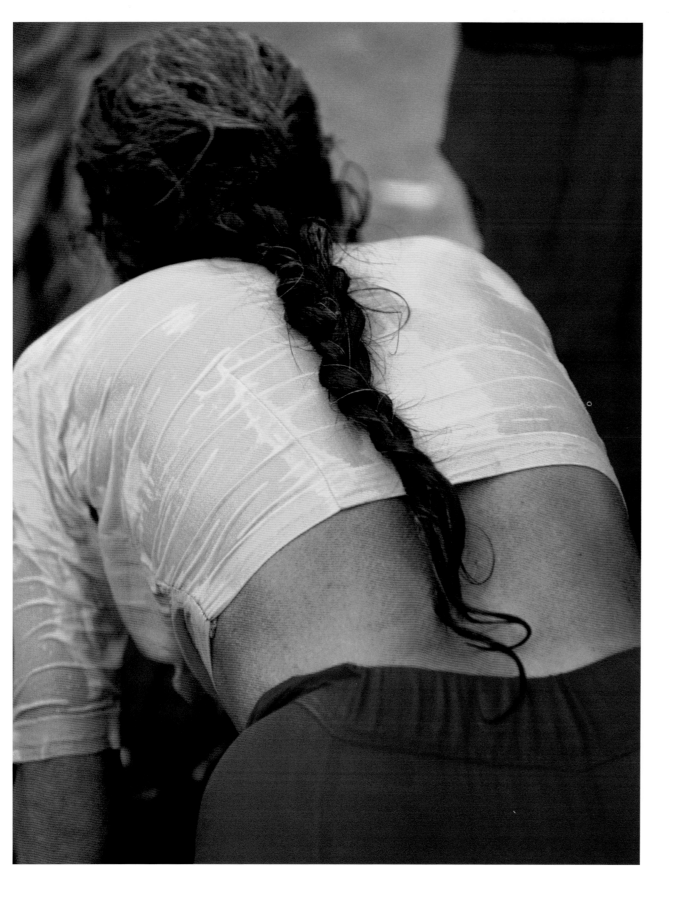

Plate 12

BOUND

China

Plate 13

WITH THIS PRAYER

Zhongdian, China

Plate 14

BOAT ON NIGER
The Niger River, Mali

Plate 15

PAGODA FOREST
Shaolin, China

« Plate 16

MINARET
Turpan, China

Plate 17 »

FALL
Silk Road, Western China

Plate 18

UIGHUR FARMER

Kashgar, Western China

Plate 19

WHITE WRAP

Morocco

Plate 20

LANTERNS
Yangshuo, China

Plate 21

THE WAIT
Forbidden City, China

Plate 22

LADLES

Tibet

Plate 23
BOATS
Morocco

Plate 24
SLIPPERS
Morocco

Plate 25 »
THREE-INCH GOLDEN LOTUS #1
China
Plate 26 »
THREE-INCH GOLDEN LOTUS #2
China

Plate 27

THRESHOLD
Shaolin Temple, China

Plate 28

QUARTERS

Morocco

Plate 32

GION

Kyoto, Japan

Plate 36

NAXI BLUE

China

Plate 37

THE GAME
Budapest, Hungary

Plate 38

THE CONVERSATION
Morocco

Plate 39

THE TANNERY
Fes, Morocco

Plate 40 »

FOUR THOUSAND MILES
China

Plate 41

WHITE HORSE

Tibet

Plate 42

ONE-THOUSAND-MILE STARE
Gansu, China

Plate 43

TIBETAN SKIRT

Namtso, Tibet

Plate 44

TRIO

Brazil

Plate 45

SITTING MONK
Bhutan

Plate 46

ENCHANTMENT

Lhasa, Tibet

Plate 47

RAYS

Kashgar, Western China

Plate 48

KEEPER OF THE HERD
The Li River, China

Plate 52

PRAYER FLAGS

Bhutan

Plate 53

HAMAR WOMAN
Ethiopia

Plate 54

GALEB

Omo Valley, Ethiopia

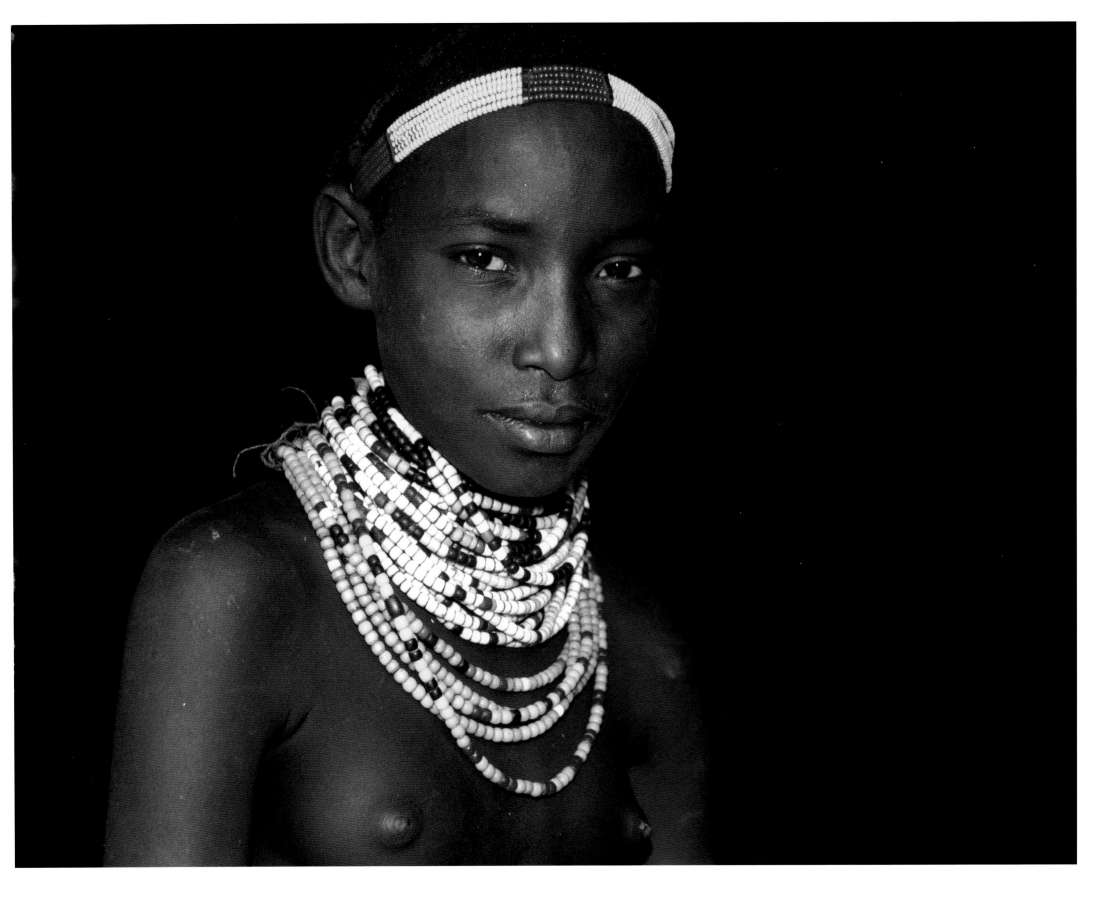

Plate 55

LILLIES

Chichicastanengo, Guatemala

Plate 56

GIFT WITHIN

Cambodia

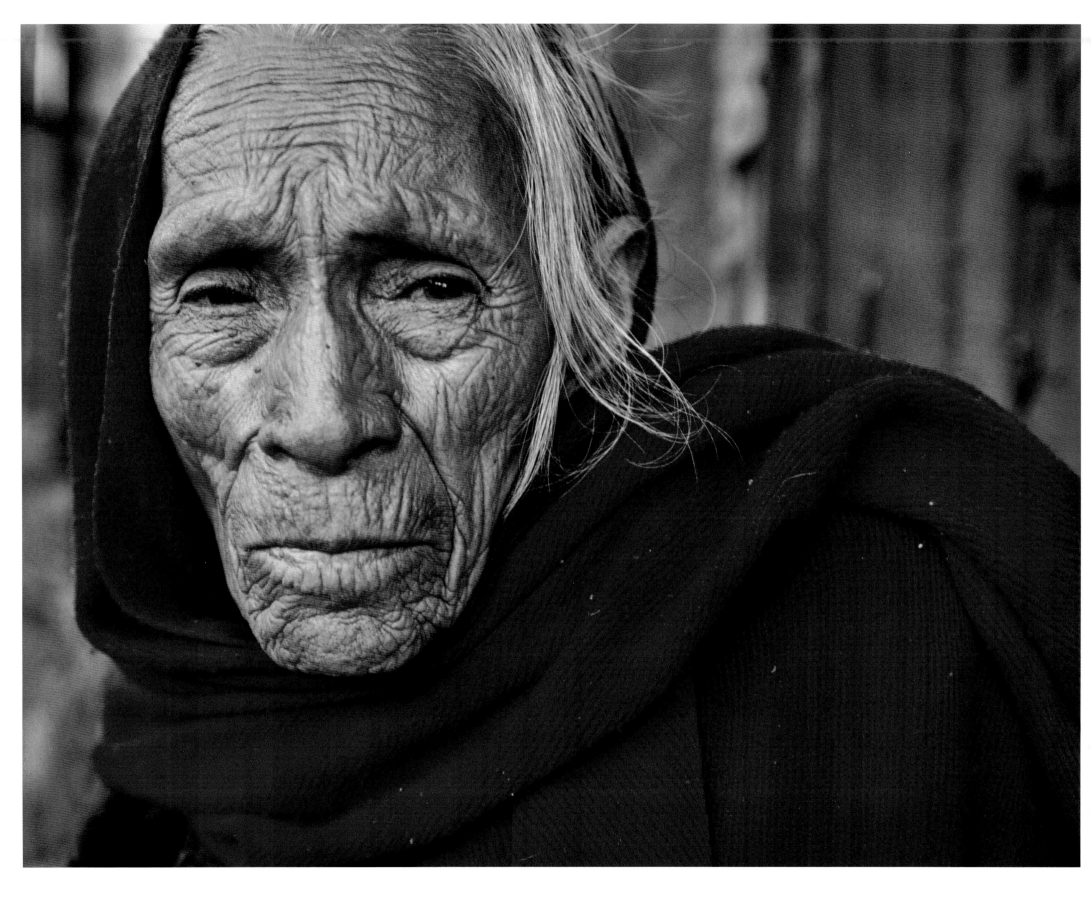

Plate 57

ELDER

Mexico

Plate 58

AFTERNOON LAUNDRY

India

Plate 59

HOLY READING

Lalibela, Ethiopia

Plate 60

TOWARD MECCA

Kashgar, Western China

Plate 61

ON WATER
India

Plate 62

SILENCE

Dzedong Nunnery, Tibet

Plate 1
HIGH PLATEAU
Himalayan Range, Tibet

The Buddhist Kingdom of Tibet, cradled in the Himalayan range at an average elevation of 16,000 feet, is known as the "roof of the world." A farmer, or *rongpa,* walks to her fields one morning, completely at home in this dramatic landscape, surrounded by the dancing, ever-changing light on the mountains.

Plate 2
DUNES
The Great Sahara, on the border of Morocco and Algeria

The Tuareg tribes, a Berber ethnic group, were dubbed the "blue men" centuries ago when their skin, hair and beards were stained a deep blue color by the impermanent dye of their indigo robes. The Tuareg have operated the trans-Saharan caravan trade for more than two millennia. Today found mostly in West Africa, the Tuareg once roamed the entire Sahara. The blue men still earn their living in trade, transporting slabs of salt—once as valuable as gold—on their camels, traveling by night to avoid heat and navigating by the stars.

Plate 3
STRIPES
Chefchouen, Rif Mountains, Morocco

This small mountain village was founded in 1471 as a base for the Rifian Berber tribes to launch attacks on the Portuguese. The town prospered and grew considerably in 1494 with the arrival of Muslim and Jewish refugees fleeing persecution in Granada.

The community remained isolated until the 1920s, when Spaniards invaded the town. Prior to this, Christians were forbidden by threat of death to enter the city. When the Spaniards arrived, they were surprised to hear a rare and old variant of medieval Castilian.

The blue dwellings typical of the village were introduced by the Jews in the 1930s, replacing the whitewashed buildings with green doors and windows, a traditional Muslim color. Today, the village is a quiet haven of steep narrow streets, blue lime-washed buildings, small squares and fountains. A woman swathed in traditional red and white Berber textiles enters her home.

Plate 4
ARCHES
Meknes, Morocco

In Islamic architecture, in what is referred to as the 'architecture of the veil,' the façade of a building is often plain while the interior is richly decorated with stonework, mosaics and calligraphy. As both a sign of humility, and the need to exclude the outside environment while protecting the private inner life, the innermost sanctum is kept hidden. A guardian watches over the inner courtyard of this mausoleum, the final resting place of Moulay Ismail, the third ruler of the Moroccan Alaouite dynasty from 1672-1727. Moulay Ismail moved the capital from Fes to Meknes and transformed it into a city that is sometimes called Versailles of Morocco for its extravagance.

Plate 5
SILVER
Northern Thailand

The Akha are a semi-nomadic tribe of Southeast Asia who make their homes on the steep slopes of high mountains. Originally from Tibet, the Akha migrated to Thailand in the past 200 years. These peoples move across national boarders, often fleeing oppression, without regard for or attachment to the particular nation in which they reside.

The Akha adorn themselves in intricate silver ornamentation and embroidered textiles. Their economy is based on rice, corn and opium. The Akha hold animist beliefs, with a emphasis on ancestral worship. Shamanism has also remained an important part of their culture.

Plate 6
LEANING POTS
India

Women decked out in bright saris and jewelry shop for cooking pots in a market.

Plate 7
BLUE MAN
Great Sahara, North Africa

The Tuareg, a nomadic Muslim tribe of the southern Sahara, are matrilineal, though not matriarchal. The most famous Tuareg symbol is the *Tagelmust,* an indigo veil. Men are veiled, but women are not. The practice of wearing the veil came from the belief that it would ward off evil spirits, although it had the practical advantage of protecting from the harsh desert sands. Men begin wearing a veil when they reach maturity; it usually conceals their entire face other than their eyes and the top of the nose.

Today, the traditional indigo turban is still preferred for celebrations, and generally Tuaregs wear clothing and turbans in a variety of colors.

Plate 8
HOLY BATHER
India

Like a river of humanity, millions of people swarm the banks of the sacred Ganges river at Allahabad to celebrate the Hindu spiritual festival of the Kumbha Mela. Devout Hindus believe that by bathing in the Ganges one is freed from their karma and thus becomes eligible for liberation from the endless cycle of birth and death. The pilgrims come from all walks of life, traveling long distances and tolerating great physical discomfort, such as sleeping in the open air in near-freezing weather.

Plate 9
BANARAS, CITY OF LIGHT
Northern India

Varanasi, the City of Light, on the banks of the Ganges river in the northern Indian state of Uttar Pradesh, is one of the oldest continually inhabited cities, dating back thousands of years. According to myth, Varanasi—also known as Banaras—was founded by the Hindu deity Shiva, thus making it one of the most important Hindu pilgrimage destinations in the country. Hindus believe that bathing in the Ganges will atone for sins and that dying in the holy city ends the cycle of rebirth.

Plate 10
MONASTERY ENTRANCE
Tibet

Tibetan Buddhist nuns live a life similar to that of monks, though less visible. Their religious practice mainly focuses on meditation and prayer rather than advanced philosophical studies. It is currently only possible for women to take *Rabjungma* ('entering') and *Getshülma* ('novice') ordinations in Tibetan tradition. With the support of the current Dalai Lama, this may soon change. The reinstatement of Gelongma lineage, which had been lost in India and Tibet for centuries, would allow women fully monastic ordination.

Plate 11

TSECHU DRUMMER
Bhutan

Nestled in the Himalayas, Bhutan is often romantically described as the last Shangri-la. The Himalayan kingdom's remoteness has been reinforced by strict tourism policies designed to protect the kingdom's pristine natural and cultural identity.

The Tsechu festival dates to the 9th century, when Guru Padmasambhava, or Guru Rinpoche, the second Buddha in Tantric Buddhism, introduced Buddhism to Tibet and Bhutan.

The royal Tsechu drummers play during the dancing rituals. It is believed that the dances were not invented by man, instead they are reproductions of celestial dances that meditation masters witnessed during deep trances.

Plate 12

BOUND
China

The Chinese custom of foot binding began in the 10th century during the Tang dynasty reign of Li Yu. According to popular legend, his favorite consort danced with her feet wrapped in silk, and the other concubines imitated her foot binding to impress the emperor. By the 12th century the practice had become widespread among the upper classes, and eventually it spread to all levels of society; it was finally outlawed in 1911.

The process of foot binding began between 4 and 7 years of age. The foot was soaked in hot water, massaged, and then wrapped so that four toes were forced under the foot, eventually breaking the arch; the big toe was left unturned for balance. This process took at least three years to complete. The result of this process was a tiny foot, ideally three inches long. A Chinese adage says: "Every pair of small feet costs a bath of tears."

Plate 13

WITH THIS PRAYER
Zhongdian, China

A woman prays at the Ganden Monastery. She circles the entire monastery everyday, reciting the sacred mantra *Om mani padme hum,* "hail to the jewel in the lotus."

Plate 14

BOAT ON NIGER
The Niger River, Mali

The Niger river snakes some 2,500 miles from its origin in Guinea up through Mali and the Sahara desert before looping back through Niger, along the border with Benin and on through Nigeria out into the Guinea sea. Old wooden pinasses and pirogue boats carry cargo along this wide, often monotonous ribbon of water, which serves as water source and highway. Its shores are often devoid of any habitation or vegetation. Villages are few and far between along the river, and are bustling with activity.

Plate 15

PAGODA FOREST
Shaolin, China

The Pagoda Forest is a clustering of more than 250 tombs of eminent monks and abbots of the nearby Shaolin Temple in Henan province, built in 495 A.D. In 527 A.D., an Indian Buddhist priest named Bodhidharma (Da Mo in Chinese) traveled to China to see the emperor. By that time, the emperor had already ordered local Buddhist monks to translate Buddhist texts from Sanskrit to Chinese. It is said that Da Mo observed Shaolin's monks spending long periods hunched over, transcribing scripture, and consequently lacking the physical and mental stamina necessary for Buddhist meditation practice. In response he created a walking meditation that imitated the natural motions of animals and birds, which evolved into a form of unarmed combat known as Kung Fu. Its pagodas dating from the late eighth century to 1803, the pagoda forest is used today for Kung Fu practice.

Plate 16

MINARET
Turpan, Xinjiang Autonomous Region, Western China

The Turpan basin is the lowest place in China and the second lowest in the world after the Dead Sea, with almost no rain and temperatures up to 120 degrees, Fahrenheit. Turpan was an important staging post along the Silk Road and was a center of Buddhism before being converted to Islam in the 8th century. Emin Minaret was built in the Afghani style in 1777 by the local ruler, Emin Hoja. The minaret is circular and the 44-meter walls are intricately carved and well preserved. The temple is still used for mass today.

Plate 17

FALL
Kashgar, Silk Road, Xinjiang Autonomous Region, Western China

Despite its isolation, Kashgar, also known as Kashi, was once the hub of the Silk Road, where desert brigands thrived and exotic bazaars full of colorful silks and other wares were traded. Kashgar is the archetypal desert oasis, lined with poplar trees—the last outpost of civilization between the vast deserts of Xinjiang and the icy peaks of the Karakoram mountains bordering Pakistan. It remains a place of pristine beauty today.

Plate 18

UIGHUR FARMER
Kashgar, Xinjiang Autonomous Region, Western China

Uighur, (pronounced "we-gar"), is an ethnic group of western Asia with a homeland in the areas of Kashgar, Urumqi and Turfan, in Xinjiang province and in the neighboring Central Asian republics. The Uighurs' ancestors were the nomadic Turkic Gaoche people and the Tocharian people of the Tarim Basin in western China. Gaoche, meaning high cart, was a reference to the distinct ox-drawn carts used to move yurts. Uighur farmers today still use these ox carts.

Kashgar, the hub city of the Silk Road, is west of the Taklamakan desert at the feet of the Tian Shan mountain range.

Plate 19

WHITE WRAP
Essaouira, Morocco

The Koran instructs Muslims to act with modesty and humility. For devout Muslim women, this requires dressing modestly to avoid drawing attention to oneself—especially features that are physically attractive and enticing to the opposite sex.

Many of the women of Essaouira dress in *haik,* the most concealing of traditional Moroccan dress. Haik consists of a large woolen or cotton sheet wrapped in such a way as to completely cover the head and body, leaving open only a narrow slit for the eyes.

Plate 20
LANTERNS
Yangshuo, near Guilin, Guangxi province, China

Passed down through the generations for 1,300 years, the traditional method of cormorant fishing in China is still practiced today. Using leashes, a fisherman controls up to a dozen birds, perched on his outstretch arms with rings around their necks to prevent them swallowing the fish they catch. Lanterns suspended over the water from the simple bamboo rafts attract the fish, which the cormorants snatch and disgorge for their handler. When they have caught enough fish, the rings are removed so the cormorants can feed. One cormorant can feed an entire family.

Plate 21
THE WAIT
The Forbidden City, China

The Fobidden City, in the center of Beijing, was home to China's emperors and was the symbolic center of the Chinese universe. Now open to the public, the palace was the exclusive domain of the Imperial Court and dignitaries. This gentleman enjoys a quiet moment in the Hall of Supreme Harmony.

Plate 22
LADLES
Tibet

The cavernous cooking areas of a monastery bustle with activity. The rooms are filled with enormous brimming pots, and the hanging ladles shimmer in the light.

Plate 23
BOATS
Essaouira, Morocco

In the 18th century, nearly half of northern Africa's Atlantic trade passed through the Moroccan port of Essaouira. Dubbed 'the port of Timbuktu,' it was the destination of sub-Saharan caravans carrying goods for export to Europe. Today the port supports some 500 families. The harbor bustles with fishermen mending nets, sorting fishhooks, and tipping cartloads of ice into grimy wooden boats, while boat builders hammer curved wooden hulls and paint them a traditional brilliant blue.

Plate 24
SLIPPERS
Meknes, Morocco

In Islamic architecture, in what is referred to as the 'architecture of the veil,' the façade of a building is often plain while the interior is richly decorated with stonework, mosaics and calligraphy. As both a sign of humility, and the need to exclude the outside environment while protecting the private inner life, the innermost sanctum is kept hidden. A guardian watches over the inner courtyard of this mausoleum, the final resting place of Moulay Ismail, the third ruler of the Moroccan Alaouite dynasty from 1672-1727.

Plate 25
THREE-INCH GOLDEN LOTUS, STUDY #1
China

Foot binding began as a fashion among the rich in China, in the 10th century. By essentially crippling a woman and rendering her unable to work, bound feet indicated her family's wealth and status. Eventually the practice spread to all levels of society, and became a prerequisite for marriage. This posed a great burden on poor families who needed their girls to work.

Li was born to a farming family, and from a young age helped her mother in the fields. When Li was eight, her mother decided it was time to begin the foot binding process. It was painful and grueling, and she remembers being unable to walk for a full winter. Li, now a charming 93-year-old great-grandmother, is nevertheless proud of her three-inch "golden lotus" feet. The binding was an essential part of her life, she told me. She had a wonderful husband and seven children, and she said none of this would be possible if she hadn't had her feet bound.

Plate 26
THREE-INCH GOLDEN LOTUS, STUDY #2
China

In a small village in southern China, I met four old women with bound feet. When asked about the purpose of foot binding, they responded very simply that without bound feet it was impossible to find a husband. When they were growing up in the early 1900s, women with unbound feet were regarded as unrefined, and often subject to ridicule. Women of the upper classes could never have imagined finding a husband of equal status without having had their feet bound as children, and a lower-class woman with unbound feet would have difficulty finding a mate—her only alternative being sold into service.

Foot binding came to be seen as an expression of cultural refinement. Viewed as the essence of feminine beauty, the tiny feet developed a sexual mystique as the most erotic and intimate part of the female anatomy. Wives, mistresses and prostitutes were chosen solely on the size and shape of their feet. Yet the foot itself was never actually on display, viewed instead wrapped in tiny, intricately embroidered lotus slippers.

Plate 27
THRESHOLD
Shaolin Temple, Henan province, China

The Shaolin Temple is credited with creating the martial art of Kung Fu, under Bodhidharma, an Indian monk who arrived in China in 527 AD. The monks who reside here follow a rigorous practice of wushu, or martial arts.

Plate 28
QUARTERS
Fes, Morocco

Fes el Bali, the walled old section of Fes, is a UNESCO World Heritage Site. Within the walls of its medina, or old city, are 9,400 pedestrian alleyways and blind turns graced with tucked-away souks, shops, mosques and theological schools called medersas. The medersas of Fes are home to some of Morocco's greatest scholars. As a residential place of learning, students immerse themselves in religious, cultural, science and Islamic arts studies.

Es Sahrij Medersa was built in 1321. The cedar carvings in this image frame the windows to students' sleeping quarters.

Plate 29
SILK SLEEVES
Labrang, China

This pilgrim wears the national dress known as *chuba*, made of wool and sheepskin, its sleeves adorned with fine silk. He has walked 100 kilometers from his home to devote himself to the *kora*, or pilgrimage paths, of the Labrang Monastery.

Large, colorful prayer wheels surround the entire monastery. The pilgrims walk clockwise around the path and turn the heavy prayer wheels so that, with each revolution, a prayer is "recited." The larger prayer wheels can hold up to a mile's worth of prayer handwritten on the rolled scrolls inside.

Plate 30
FIVE MONKS
Drepung Monastery, Tibet

Drepung monastery, founded in 1416, is the largest in Tibet and at its peak housed some 10,000 monks. The massive assembly hall, or Tsogchen, in this image is supported by 108 pillars and gently lit by filtered sunshine and pungent yak-butter lamps. Throughout the day monks gather for recitations and chanting of the Holy Scriptures.

Plate 31
THIS MOMENT
Drepung Monastery, Tibet

See above.

Plate 32
GION
Kyoto, Japan

A maiko is an apprentice *geisha,* or hostess. During their rigorous apprenticeship, which can last for five or six years, maiko train under their geisha mentor. The *one-san/imoto-san* (older–junior) relationship is extremely important. The geisha will teach the maiko the most refined social and entertaining skills—how to properly serve tea, dance, play the shamisen, and converse.

In the 1920s there were more than 80,000 geisha in Japan. Today the exact number, while unknown to outsiders, is estimated at less than 2,000, primarily in the Gion and Pontocho districts of Kyoto.

Plate 33
DRYING SARIS
Allahabad, India

The sari has many names, forms and uses in various parts of the country. Four feet wide and anywhere from 13 to 26 feet long, this fluid garment is draped around the body in myriad ways, a picture of flowing grace that conceals as much as it reveals.

Plate 34
AFRICAN SILK
Northern Territory, Kenya

The tribes of East Africa are renowned for their physical beauty and attention to detail in daily dress. It is not at all unusual to see young men and women dressed in bright cloth and extravagantly adorned in intricate beadwork. These young girls are from the Samburu tribe, whose women commonly wear their hair short while men sport long plaits.

Plate 35
HAMAR
Ethiopia

The Hamar people in Ethiopia are known for their practice of wearing a multitude of colorful beads. The women are graceful, with long, braided hair, and adorn their necks with polished iron jewelry. Their backs are covered with scars, considered the sign of a true Hamar woman, that they receive in a ritual beating. Women marry young, typically to much older men, and widows may not remarry; thus women commonly end up as heads of families. They also control the property of their dead husband's younger brothers if his parents are gone.

Plate 36
NAXI BLUE
Lijiang, China

The Naxi ethnic group, based in the town of Lijiang in Yunnan province, numbers some 278,000. Naxi are easily recognizable with their blue blouses and trousers covered by blue or black aprons. Until recently, the Naxi lived in matriarchal families, although local rulers were always male. Their society still maintains matriarchal practices, with flexible living arrangements for couples. Partners live in their own homes, and children born to the couple are raised by the woman. The father provides support, but if the relationship ends, so does the support; no special effort is made to recognize paternity. Women inherit all property, and female elders adjudicate disputes.

Plate 37
THE GAME
Budapest, Hungary

Hungary is home to more than 100 thermal bathhouses of fine Ottoman architecture, with octagonal pools, cupolas and colored glass windows and perhaps the most unique and hedonistic bathing experience offered in history. From the Danube river, which follows the fault line separating the Buda Hills from a great plain, some 40 million liters of warm mineral water gush forth daily from 120 springs.

The palace-like edifice of the Széchenyi Baths contains a huge thermal pool where men often play chess on floating boards while immersed in mineral water valued for its medicinal properties.

Plate 38
THE CONVERSATION
Essaouira, Morocco

The seaport of Essaouira is one of the most enchanted villages in all of Morocco. Inside the ramparts, filled with white-walled houses with sky-blue paintwork, women seem to float through its covered alleyways, enveloped in *haiks*—white voluminous shrouds that cover everything except their sandals and colorful socks.

Plate 39
THE TANNERY
Fes, Morocco

Tanning is one of the world's oldest traditional livelihoods, dating back more than 7,000 years. In a series of procedures, including hair removal, soaking, drying and rinsing, animal hides are transformed into soft, rot-proof leather, before being handed over to leather workers. Some of the ingredients in this odorous process include pigeon excrement, cow urine, fish oils, animal fats and brains, chromium salts, and sulphuric acids.

Little changed from their medieval origins, tanneries are still constructed from mud brick and tile, and the finished skins hauled to the market by donkey. Health and safety for the workers in the tanning pits has changed little over the centuries, and the structure under which the craftsmen and apprentices are organized is according to medieval guild principles. Fassi leather, made in the Wadi Fes, has for centuries been considered amongst the finest in the world.

Plate 40
FOUR THOUSAND MILES
Jin Shan Ling, China

The Great Wall of China is actually is a series of stone and earthen fortifications, built between the 5th century BCE and the 17th century AD by successive dynasties to protect the northern borders of the Chinese empire. Little remains of the most famous section, built between 220 and 200 BCE by the first emperor of China, Qin Shi Huang. The existing wall, built by the Ming Dynasty in the 15th century of stone and brick, is the world's longest man-made structure, stretching some 3,950 miles from Shanghai Pass in the east to Lop Nur in the west, along an arc that roughly delineates the southern edge of Inner Mongolia.

Plate 41

WHITE HORSE
Tibet

The nomads of Tibet, called Drokpas, travel in groups of several families. Each family lives in a small yak-skin tent, passed down from generation to generation. The Drokpas migrate as often as ten times per year, following a route as they graze their livestock through the summer months into late autumn. By early winter, the herd is usually fattened and ready for the onset of snow. The nomads believe their livestock are sacred, bestowed upon them by the gods. They are also an important part of their livelihood.

The Drokpas endure bitter winters, camping at altitudes up to 15,000 feet. They often make pilgrimages to monasteries throughout Tibet, prostrating themselves along the journey, which may be hundreds of miles. They bring meat, butter and salt to trade in the markets at various destinations.

Plate 42

ONE-THOUSAND-MILE STARE
Gansu, China

The nomad's entire life is spent among rugged high mountains. He is constantly moving with his family and livestock, but also spending much time alone.

Plate 43

TIBETAN SKIRT
Namtso, Tibet

Tibet's high altitude and harsh climate give its children their ruddy cheeks. This boy clings to his mother's striped apron, which indicates she is married.

Plate 44

TRIO
The Amazon, Brazil

The Amazon is home to 60 percent of Brazil's indigenous population, which numbered about five million people when Europeans arrived in 1500. For centuries, the Amazon acted as a natural barrier, protecting its jungle inhabitants from European colonizers. Today there are 210 nations speaking 170 languages and known dialects. They add up to a total population of about 300,000, and are scattered

over thousands of villages throughout Brazil. There are still at least 50 indigenous tribes in the Brazilian Amazon that have not come into contact with outsiders.

The children of the Amazon, when not in school, spend much of their day playing with monkeys, lounging in hammocks, eating Cupuaçu fruit, running naked, their bodies painted blue with dye from the Jenipapo tree.

Plate 45

SITTING MONK
Bhutan

Novices can join monasteries as young as five years old. They start their training by learning to chant the holy texts.

Plate 46

ENCHANTMENT
Lhasa, Tibet

At Lhasa's Buddhist Jokhang temple, one of the oldest and most sacred temples in Tibet, this young child has arrived with her family on pilgrimage. In a country of few roads or motorized vehicles, Tibetans walk long distances to holy sites, in order to accumulate merit or good luck.

Plate 47

RAYS
Kashgar, Western China

Kashgar is a important hub on the old Silk Road, and a vibrant Islamic center. It is the largest oasis city in Chinese Central Asia and its population is 90 percent Uighur. These boys are responsible for cutting the meat in the local cookhouse.

Plate 48

KEEPER OF THE HERD
The Li River, Guanxi province, China

The Li, or Lijiang river, in northeastern Guangxi province has long been famous for its limestone karst hills. This tranquil, crystal-clear river is also home to bamboo groves, rice fields, picturesque villages, and water buffalo grazing by the water's edge. Peasant farmers here till their land as their ancestors did, by hand and with animals, and rely on most of their crop to feed their families.

Plate 49

PEMA'S SECRET
Zhongdian, China

Tibetan women from the region of Zhongdian renowned for their beauty, traditionally wear a fuchsia headpiece. The girl's silk garment is an ordinary outfit. In Buddhist fashion, her hair is braided in 108 plaits.

Plate 50

JOB'S TEARS
The Highlands, Papua New Guinea

The Highlands of Papua New Guinea, thanks to its remote location, remains quite traditional, especially in terms of clan and tribal loyalties.

This wife is in mourning, thus covered in the gray clay according to Asaro tribal custom. While she is in mourning, she will be adorned with numerous threads of seeds known as "Job's tears." One string is removed each day until, at last, with the removal of the final cord, the widow will wash herself of the grey earth and be released from mourning.

Plate 51

THE APPLICATION
The Highlands, Papua New Guinea

A "sing-sing" is a word for celebration in the Papuan language, and can be held for any number of reasons such as the birth of a child, the winning of a battle or celebrating a sacred day. A warrior prepares himself, carefully applying his make-up.

Plate 52

PRAYER FLAGS
Bhutan

Prayer flags are everywhere in Bhutan, waving from mountain passes, monasteries, rooftops and meadows. Legend says they ensure prayer with each flutter. Unlike Tibetan prayer flags, which are strung together and hang between buildings or hilltops, Bhutanese prayer flags are attached to tall poles and bunched together like colorful trees.

Plate 53

HAMAR WOMAN
Ethiopia

The Hamar people in Ethiopia are known for their practice of wearing a multitude of colorful beads. The women are graceful, with long, braided hair, and adorn their necks with polished iron jewelry.

Plate 54

GALEB
Omo Valley, Ethiopia

The Galeb tribe inhabits a dry and desolate area of southwest Ethiopia, in the delta of the Omo River, in villages spread over numerous islands.

Plate 55

LILLIES
Chichicastanengo, Guatemala

The ancient Mayan civilization, considered one of the grandest in history, occupied a vast geographic area in Central and South America from around 2000 BCE until 1500 AD.

Today descendents of the old Maya, known locally as the indigenous, account for more than half of the Guatemalan population. Their vibrant culture is thriving, as evidenced by the many traditionally dressed woman and children throughout the country. Twice a week Mayans, with bundles of goods on their backs, stream down the cobblestone streets to the center square of Chichicastanengo, where the largest indigenous market continues to take place.

Plate 56

GIFT WITHIN
Cambodia

Theravada Buddhism is the predominant religion of ethnic Khmer, representing 90 percent of the Cambodian population. Women are not ordained, but older women, especially widows, can become nuns. They live in wats, or temples, shave their heads and eyebrows, and generally follow the same precepts as monks.

Plate 57

ELDER
San Miguel, Mexico

From colorful textiles, costumes and traditional crafts to the agricultural calendar and communalist social organization, pre-colonial traditions still hold sway among Mexico's surviving indigenous people.

Plate 58

AFTERNOON LAUNDRY
Allahabad, India

Laundry in India is truly beautiful to see. The drying of saris is often done by two women holding each end, allowing the breeze to warm and dry the thin cloth. The cloth blows in the wind like an enormous, brightly colored ribbon.

Plate 59

HOLY READING
Lalibela, Ethiopia

At an altitude of 8,500 feet, the spiritual village of Lalibela sits on a volcanic rock terrace. People of this region are devout Orthodox Christians. The churches are sunken into the earth so that the rooftops are level with the ground. They have grottos, crypts and courtyards, many of which are interconnected by catacombs and labyrinthine passageways.

Plate 60

TOWARD MECCA
Kashgar, Xinjiang Autonomous Region, China

Within two centuries after its rise in the 7th century, Islam spread from its original home in Arabia into Syria, Egypt, North Africa, and Spain to the west, and into Persia, India, and, by the end of the 10th century, into western China.

Devout Muslims pray five times daily, always facing Mecca—the city in Saudi Arabia where Muslims believe the first house of worship to God was built.

Plate 61

ON WATER
Ganges River, India

Like a river of humanity, millions of people swarm the banks of the sacred Ganges river at Allahabad to celebrate the Hindu spiritual festival of the Kumbha Mela. Devout Hindus believe that by bathing in the Ganges one is freed from their karma and thus becomes eligible for liberation from the endless cycle of birth and death. The pilgrims come from all walks of life, traveling long distances and enduring great discomfort, such as sleeping in the open air in extremely cold weather.

Plate 62

SILENCE
Dzedong Nunnery, Tibet

Buddhism infuses every aspect of Tibetans' life. Most nuns have spent their young lives as farm girls, growing barley and wheat, tending yak and sheep, and caring for younger children, before choosing a life of celibacy, study and religious devotion.

The deep, eerie sound of chanting emanates from the assembly hall, where monks gather for hours or days at a "sitting" to chant mantras and sutras. Mantras, meaning "protection of the mind," are chants used during meditation to help transform consciousness. Sutras are classic discourses of the Buddha.

TECHNICAL NOTES

The equipment I use to create my work is an all-analogue cameras, with focus, aperture and shutter speed set manually. The majority of images seen here have been made with a K.B. Canham 4x5" field view camera, with Nikkor lenses ranging in focal length from 135mm to 500mm. Otherwise the photographs have been created using medium-and small-format cameras, using lenses from 65mm to 150mm and 35mm to 70mm respectively. I use a Sekonic L-508 light meter.

A variety of transparency films, both rolls and sheets, are used—each of which is selected depending on lighting conditions, altitude, temperature and subject matter. I use a carbon-fiber Gitzo G1376M.

I do not use artificial flash or filters as I find ambient light utterly beautiful and sensual. The color found in my images is created in the field when the exposure is made. When I print my work, I make every effort to match the rich, vibrant color of the original transparency.

My images are made as candids with the exception of a few select images, such as the women with bound feet, who were very old and I wanted to be comfortable. For portraiture, I do not use telephoto lenses. I prefer to be intimate with my subject and find the nearness of the person to be enchanting; this evokes a stronger image.

For the past 17 years I had been hand-printing my images using Ilfochrome (Cibachrome) processing, but due to its recent unavailability, I now print my work using Fuji Crystal Archive processing. This archival paper is processed through traditional wet chemistry, boasting a brilliant presentation and ensuring a long life span.